Drake → Duck ←

Two mallards

A flock of wild geese flying south in a V shape

← Here are some feathers that make up a kestrel's wing.

Baby blue tits in a tree nest

The guillemot's egg is pear-shaped.

Birds

Written by Jill Bailey and David Burnie

Consultant: Ben Hoare

DK

Penguin Random House

Senior editor Gill Pitts
Editor Olivia Stanford
Assistant editor Kritika Gupta
Editorial assistance Cécile Landau
US Senior editor Margaret Parrish
Senior art editor Ann Cannings
Art editor Rashika Kachroo
Illustrators Abby Cook, Dan Crisp, Shahid Mahmood
Jacket co-ordinator Francesca Young
Jacket designers Dheeraj Arora, Amy Keast, Faith Nelson
DTP designers Vijay Kandwal, Mohd. Rizwan, Dheeraj Singh

Picture researcher Sakshi Saluja
Producer, pre-production Dragana Puvacic
Producer Isabell Schart
Managing editors Soma B. Chowdhury,
Laura Gilbert, Monica Saigal
Managing art editors Neha Ahuja Chowdhry,
Diane Peyton Jones
Art director Martin Wilson
Publisher Sarah Larter
Publishing director Sophie Mitchell

Original edition
Senior editor Susan McKeever
Art editor Vicky Wharton
Editor Jodi Block
Senior art editor Jacquie Gulliver
Production Catherine Semark
Editorial consultant Peter Colston, The British Museum (Natural History), Tring.
Illustrators Diana Catchpole, Angelika Elsebach, Jane Gedye, Nick Hewetson, Ruth Lindsay,
Louis Mackay, Polly Noakes, Lorna Turpin

First American Edition, 1992
This edition published in the United States in 2017 by
DK Publishing, 345 Hudson Street, New York, New York 10014

Copyright © 1992, 1997, 2017 Dorling Kindersley Limited
DK, a Division of Penguin Random House LLC
17 18 19 20 21 10 9 8 7 6 5 4 3 2 1
001–298510–Apr/2017

A catalog record for this book is available from the Library of Congress.
ISBN 978-1-4654-5757-8

DK books are available at special discounts when purchased in bulk for sales promotions, premiums, fund-raising, or educational use.
For details, contact: DK Publishing SpecialMarkets, 345 Hudson Street, New York, New York 10014 SpecialSales@dk.com

Printed and bound in China.

The publisher would like to thank the following for their kind permission to reproduce their photographs:
(Key: a-above; b-below/bottom; c-center; f-far; l-left; r-right; t-top)
4 123RF.com: Delmas Lehman (cra). **5 iStockphoto.com:** Roger Whiteway. **7 Corbis:** Frits van Daalen / NiS / Minden Pictures (b). **8 Getty Images:** Koki Iino (cla). **13 123RF.com:** Michael
Mill (tr). **17 123RF.com:** Renamarie (clb). **18 iStockphoto.com:** pum_eva (cr). **19 Alamy Stock Photo:** Nature Picture Library (cra). **Dreamstime.com:** Ajdibilio (cla). **20 Corbis:** DLILLC
(bl). **21 Corbis:** Tim Laman / National Geographic Creative (tr). **22 Dorling Kindersley:** Natural History Museum, London (cra). **25 123RF.com:** Anna Yakimova (tl).
27 123RF.com: Witold Kaszkin (cla). **28 123RF.com:** Vladimir Seliverstov (bl). **Dreamstime.com:** Liqiang Wang (tr). **29 123RF.com:** Michael Lane (tr). **Alamy Stock Photo:** Duncan Usher
(br). **Dreamstime.com:** Barbara Zimmermann (cl). **30 123RF.com:** Juho Salo (cra). **33 123RF.com:** Dmytro Pylypenko (clb); Michael Lane (cr). **iStockphoto.com:** William Sherman (t).
34 iStockphoto.com: Roger Whiteway (l). **35 123RF.com:** Michael Lane (cla). **36 123RF.com:** Dave Montreuil (clb). **Alamy Stock Photo:** Dave Watts (c). **38 Alamy Stock Photo:** Dave
Watts (crb). **Dorling Kindersley:** The National Birds of Prey Centre, Gloucestershire (bc). **39 123RF.com:** Christian Musat (br); Jose Manuel Gelpi Diaz (t). **40 Dorling Kindersley:** British
Wildlife Centre, Surrey, UK. **40-41 123RF.com:** Snike (t). **41 Dorling Kindersley:** Natural History Museum, London (cra). **42 123RF.com:** Steve Byland (clb). **Alamy Stock Photo:** Keith M
Law (cra). **43 iStockphoto.com:** Paul Vinten (tr). **44 123RF.com:** Delmas Lehman (cra). **45 123RF.com:** Berka (cr). **Dreamstime.com:** Dennis Jacobsen (bl). **46 Alamy Stock Photo:** Kevin
Maskell (b). **47 123RF.com:** David Tyrer (ca, crb); Ewan Chesser (clb). **Fotolia:** Gail Johnson (cr). **48 123RF.com:** Dave Montreuil (crb). **49 123RF.com:** Abi Warner (tr); Feathercollector
(cla). **SuperStock:** age fotostock (b). **51 123RF.com:** Panu Ruangjan (cra); Steve Byland (br). **Alamy Stock Photo:** Wildlife GmbH (cl). **52 Getty Images:** Alice Cahill (crb). **53 Alamy
Stock Photo:** Rolf Nussbaumer Photography (r). **Corbis:** Frits van Daalen / NiS / Minden Pictures (b). **54 123RF.com:** Alta Oosthuizen
(bl). **55 123RF.com:** Gleb Ivanov (tl). **Dorling Kindersley:** The National Birds of Prey Centre (cra). **57 123RF.com:** Vasin Leenanuruksa (clb). **58 123RF.com:** Vasiliy Vishnevskiy (crb)

Cover images: **Front: 123RF.com:** Steve Byland (clb); **Dreamstime.com:** Brebca (crb), Mikelane45 (tc), Mustafanc (cla); **iStockphoto.com:** BMacKenziePhotography (tr);
Back: Dorling Kindersley: Barnabas Kindersley, Natural History Museum, London (crb)

All other images © Dorling Kindersley
For further information see: www.dkimages.com

A WORLD OF IDEAS:
SEE ALL THERE IS TO KNOW
www.dk.com

Contents

Looking at birds

You may not always notice birds, but they are all over the place—in the yard, by the seashore, in the city. If you become a birdwatcher, soon you will begin to learn all kinds of things about birds—how they feed, how they fly, and the different sounds that they make.

House sparrow

This busy bird is found in backyards and cities across the world. You can recognize the male by its brown back, gray crown, and black bib.

Gray crown

Black bib

Dressed for the part

When watching birds, wear dull colors so that you don't stand out too much from the background. Make sure you have some warm, waterproof clothing in case it gets cold or wet.

No bird likes noise, so be as quiet as you can when watching birds!

HOW TO DRAW A BIRD

The best way to remember a bird you see is to draw it. It is easier than you think to draw a bird. Build up your sketch from simple shapes.

1. Draw two circles—one for the head and one for the body.

2. Add the neck, beak, and legs.

3. Fill in the pattern of the feathers next.

1. Use half a circle for the body of a waterbird.

1. When drawing a bird in flight, start with two circles.

2. Add the wings, tail, neck, and beak. Is the head held out or tucked in?

3. Add in the wing details.

9

What is a bird?

Birds come in many shapes and sizes, but there are things that unite them. All birds are covered in feathers for warmth. They all have two wings, although not all birds can fly. All birds have beaks and lay eggs, and their legs and feet are covered in small scales.

Long, sharp beaks are good for finding food in soil or vegetation.

Birds have many feathers.

A bird's hollow, lightweight beak is made of horny material, and it is very strong.

Spotting starlings

There are about 10,000 species of bird, and each one has its own special features. You can identify a starling by its shiny black feathers mixed with a purple or green sheen. In winter, its feathers are speckled white.

Underneath its skin

Here is a starling without its skin! You have lots of bones under your skin, too. But a bird's bones contain many air spaces. These make the bones light for flying. A bird has very long legs—so what looks like its knees are really its ankles.

Ankle

The starling has a big keel, or breast bone. The powerful muscles that make wings beat are attached to this bone.

BIRD BEAKS

Birds have no hands, so they use their beaks to preen, build nests, and to pick up or tear up food. Different beaks are suited to eating different foods.

FANCY FOOTWORK

Birds may use their feet for perching in trees, running, or swimming. Some birds use their feet to catch prey.

Many birds that live in lakes and rivers have webbed feet for paddling.

Many ducks feed by dabbling. They open and shut their beaks to take in water and strain out food.

Goshawks are meat-eaters. They have strong, hooked beaks for tearing apart flesh.

The feet of birds of prey have long claws for gripping their prey.

The greenfinch is a seed-eater, so its short, thick beak is strong enough to crack open hard seeds.

Perching birds have one toe that points backward to grasp branches.

Feathered friends

Birds are the only animals with feathers. A large bird, such as a swan, may have more than 25,000 feathers, and even a tiny hummingbird has almost 1,000. Feathers keep birds warm and dry and allow them to fly. A bird's feathers come in many beautiful colors and shapes.

Primary feathers provide the main power for flying.

The alula prevents stalling in flight. The kestrel's unusually large alula lets it fly well at very low speeds.

Secondary feathers are curved to make air flow up under the wing, lifting the bird.

Coverts cover the base of other feathers, making a smooth surface for air to flow over.

Kestrel wing

Here are some feathers that make up a kestrel's wing. You can see the wing in action on the opposite page. Feathers grow from a central hollow rod called a quill.

Feather forms

A kestrel uses its long wing and tail feathers for flying. As it beats its wings down, the kestrel spreads its feathers out to press against the air. Like all birds, it has other feathers that are not used for flight. Smaller feathers cover the rest of the body, making it waterproof and windproof. Fluffy down feathers underneath keep the bird warm.

Hanging out to dry

A cormorant squeezes the air out of its feathers so it can dive and travel under water more easily, in search of fish. Afterward, it spends a long time with its wings spread, drying them out.

Tail feathers act as a rudder for steering. They can also be lowered and spread out to act as a brake.

FINDING FEATHERS

Start collecting any feathers that you find in the yard, on the beach, or in the woods. Fix them to paper with tape, or put them in clear plastic wallets. Make notes about where and when you found them, and label as many as possible.

Soft fringes on the edges of an owl's feathers muffle any noise made by the wings in flight, as it approaches a mouse.

The down at the base of a buzzard's coverts keeps it warm.

Taking to the air

A bird stays in the air by flapping its wings. As it pulls its wings down, the feathers push against the air, moving the bird up and forward.

The feathers twist to let air through as the wings rise.

Fast fliers

Pigeons are powerful and speedy fliers. They are good at taking off in a hurry, and can fly for many hours without a break. Some pigeons are specially trained for racing. You can recognize racing pigeons because they often have rings around their legs, showing who they belong to.

With a few flaps, it is airborne.

Silent flight

Compared to the pigeon, the barn owl has broad wings and a slow, silent flight. It flaps its way over fields and hedges, watching and listening for small animals. Because it is so quiet, it can swoop onto prey without giving itself away.

The owl springs into the air with a kick of its feet.

The wings of this city pigeon are as high as they will go, and the feathers are spread apart.

As the pigeon pulls its wings downward, the feathers flatten out to make a single surface.

The feathers separate as the wings begin to rise again. They start to flick upward, ready for the next beat of the wings.

Happy landing

Landing safely is an important part of flying. The bird has to slow down at just the right time so that it drops gently to the ground. Young birds have to practice before they can land properly.

The owl's broad wings allow it to fly slowly but still stay in the air.

When the owl spots a mouse or vole, it starts to drop, using its wings as brakes, and swings its legs down.

Legs and feet are extended, ready to seize prey.

Patterns in the air

When you see a bird in flight, notice the pattern it makes. Different kinds of birds fly in different ways. Large heavy birds, such as ducks, flap their wings all the time. Many smaller birds save their energy by gliding between flaps. Some birds hover in the air as they search for prey or feed at flowers.

A fulmar's long, narrow wings help it to glide.

Gliding

The fulmar soars upward on the rising air currents that form when the wind blowing from the sea meets the cliffs. Then it glides slowly down across the sea. It can travel a long way without flapping its wings at all.

Look for birds gliding near sea cliffs.

Hovering

The kestrel beats its wings forward and spreads its tail feathers to hover. Doing this, it can spot small rodents, such as voles or mice, on the ground below. Look for kestrels hovering over grass by the roadside or patches of rough grassland.

Tail fanned out for balance

Large wings and powerful flight muscles lift the heavy body.

If you spot a mallard flying over open ground, it is probably on its way to a lake or a river.

The mallard sticks its neck out when it flies.

Straight line
Ducks, such as mallards, and geese often fly in V formation or in straight lines, beating their wings all the time.

DRAWING FLIGHT PATTERNS

Quick sketches of a bird's flight can help to identify the bird, even if it is a long way off. Draw an outline of the shape the bird makes in flight, then indicate the way it flies with arrows.

From soaring to bounding

Meat-eating birds often need to fly long distances in search of a meal. To save energy, they soar (glide) on air currents. Many smaller birds do not need to fly so far. Some keep close to hedges and trees, where their enemies will not spot them.

Soaring

Eagles and vultures soar on thermals (warm bubbles of rising air), so they don't have to flap their wings much. In this way, they can keep an eye on the ground, and prey, and save energy as well!

Tail is fanned out.

Where do they soar?

Soaring birds go where the thermals are—over mountains, canyons, and wide open plains.

The California condor can glide for hours with its huge wings.

Hummingbirds hover in front of flowers as they sip the sweet nectar. The nectar in flowers gives the hummingbirds energy.

Flying backward

Hummingbirds live in the Americas, and are the only birds that can fly sideways, forward, and backward. They are also the best hoverers of all. They need to hover to feed on nectar from flowers.

Stooping

The peregrine falcon swoops on other smaller birds in a vertical dive known as a stoop. Spot the skydiver near cliffs or tall buildings in towns.

Bounding

Blue tits and many other small birds have a slightly bounding flight. They flap their wings in short bursts, then rest and glide. This saves energy.

Although this flight pattern is slightly exaggerated, small birds look as if they are bouncing up and down on the end of elastic!

Blue tits close their wings in between bursts of flapping.

Finding a mate

Before it can breed, a bird has to find a partner. Courtship is the way of attracting a mate that is of the right age and sex, and, most important, of the same type. Usually, the male attracts the female. If she is impressed by his courtship behavior or his bright colors, she will mate with him and lay eggs.

Red balloon

Frigatebirds spend most of their lives flying high up over the sea. They nest on tropical islands. Each male bird picks a site for the nest, and then attracts a mate by blowing up his special pouch.

The male has a pouch of stretchy skin on the front of his throat. When the female comes near, he blows up his pouch, rattles his beak against it, and flaps his wings.

A frigatebird's wings are wider than the height of a man.

Hanging around

The male blue bird-of-paradise attracts a mate by opening his wings and tipping forward until he is hanging upside down by his feet. This bird lives in tropical rain forests in New Guinea. Many other species in its family also have spectacular courtship displays.

When the male hangs upside down, his dazzling blue feathers open up like a fan.

Friend or foe?

These Arctic terns look as though they are fighting over a fish. But they are courting. The male offers his partner the fish as a gift. The two birds then fly off together calling.

Bird bonding

Once the terns have landed, the female must accept the fish from the male one last time. This shows that she is willing to pair up. Many male birds give their partners food when they are courting. This helps to make a bond between the pair.

Eggs and hatching

A bird's egg is a living package protected by a hard shell. When it is newly laid, the egg contains just the yolk and the clear part. The parent keeps the egg warm by sitting on it, or "incubating" it. The yolk nourishes the growing bird, and after a few weeks it is ready to hatch.

One of a kind
Many guillemot eggs have spots or streaks. Parents can recognize their own egg by its unique pattern.

Jungle giant
The cassowary is a huge flightless bird from tropical forests in New Guinea and Australia. The female lays up to six enormous eggs.

Blue egg

The American robin lays about four blue eggs.

Ground nester
The curlew nests on the ground. Its speckled eggs are well camouflaged.

Tiny eggs
A hummingbird's nest has enough room for two pea-sized eggs.

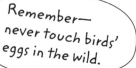

Remember— never touch birds' eggs in the wild.

Into the outside world

If you tap an egg with a spoon, its shell will quickly break. However, imagine how hard the same job is for a baby bird. It has to break the shell from the inside. It has a special egg tooth on the top of its bill, so it can chip through the shell. Here you can see how a duckling breaks out.

3. Pushing away
Once the circle is complete, the duckling gives a big heave by trying to straighten its neck. As the crack widens, one of its wings pops out.

1. Making a hole
The duckling's hardest task comes first. Using its beak, it chips away at the blunt end of the egg until it has made a hole. Then it rests.

2. Round and round
Next, the duckling hammers away at the shell. It turns all the time, so that it cuts in a circle.

4. Off with the top
Suddenly, the blunt end of the egg comes away as the duckling gives a final push.

5. Breaking out
The duckling falls out of the egg. Its wet feathers cling together, making it look bedraggled.

6. Drying off
Within two or three hours, the duckling's feathers have dried out and turned fluffy. It cannot fly yet, but it can run around and is ready for its first swim.

The first days

A duckling can feed itself when it is just a day old. But not all birds are like this. Many are blind and helpless when they hatch, and they rely on their parents to bring food to them. For adult blue tits, this means many days of hard work.

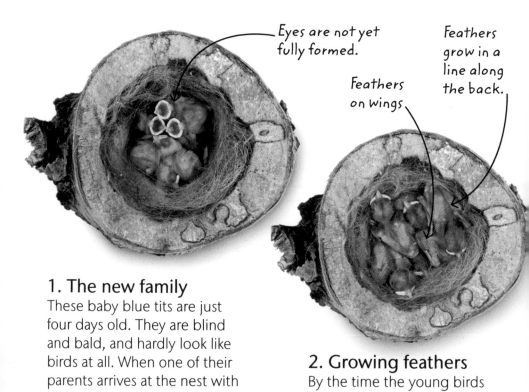

Eyes are not yet fully formed.

Feathers on wings

Feathers grow in a line along the back.

1. The new family
These baby blue tits are just four days old. They are blind and bald, and hardly look like birds at all. When one of their parents arrives at the nest with food, they open their beaks wide and stretch upward.

2. Growing feathers
By the time the young birds are six days old, their feathers have started to grow.

Many baby birds have special colored patterns inside their mouths. These show the parents where to put the food.

By the time they are ready to fly, many young birds are heavier than their parents. They are so big that they can hardly fit in the nest.

Eyes are fully open.

Wing feathers are protected by waxy tubes.

Eyes are beginning to open.

Tips of wing feathers are beginning to appear.

3. Fast food
The baby birds are now nine days old. Their parents bring them food almost once a minute, and so the nestlings quickly put on weight.

4. Growing up
Thirteen days after hatching, the nestlings are starting to look like their parents. Within a week, their wing and tail feathers will be fully grown, and they will be ready to fly.

The first flight

Baby birds know how to fly naturally, so they do not have to learn to fly. However, they do need to practice in order to learn how to twist and turn in the air, and how to land without falling on their faces.

A baby chaffinch makes its first flight, as its parents call out to encourage it.

Follow the leader

At first, baby chaffinches stay safely hidden among the branches near their nest. After a few days, they can fly quite well. Then the young birds follow their parents around as they hunt for food. This saves the parents time and energy, since they no longer have to carry food back to the nest.

Its flight feathers are not fully grown.

Brave babies

Little auks nest in the Arctic on cliff ledges high above the sea, where most of their enemies cannot reach them. On their very first flight, the baby auks must reach the sea below. There they will learn how to catch fish to eat. If they don't reach the sea, they will crash-land on the rocks.

Look out below!

The mandarin duck lays her eggs in a tree hole high above the ground, out of reach of foxes and other enemies. Before the ducklings are a day old, they must leap out of the tree. Their mother waits on the ground below, calling to them to follow her. When they have all landed safely, she will lead them to water and food.

Before landing, the baby chaffinch lowers its wing and tail to slow down. It then lowers its legs to absorb the shock as it hits the ground.

Mandarin ducklings spread their tiny wings and feet to slow their fall. Amazingly, they manage to land without getting hurt.

Good parents

Most new parents have to work very hard when a baby arrives, and birds are no exception. Newborn birds are usually helpless, so their parents have to feed them, keep them clean, and guard them against other animals that may want to eat them. Most parent birds tuck the chicks under their feathers to keep them warm or to shade them from the hot sun.

Egg imposter
European cuckoo parents avoid looking after their young by laying their eggs in other birds' nests. When the baby cuckoo hatches, it pushes the others out of the nest. This cuckoo is bigger than its foster parents, but they continue to feed it.

Penguin parents
Penguins come ashore to rear their chicks. However, they need to travel far out to sea to hunt for fish or other marine prey. The parents take turns looking after the chick. One parent stays with the chick while the other goes out to sea to fish.

Penguin parents look after their chicks until they grow a coat of stiff waterproof feathers.

The penguin chick has a thick fluffy coat, but it still huddles against its parent to keep warm.

Light as a feather

Swans lay their eggs in big nests on riverbanks. Baby swans can swim and find their own food soon after they hatch. They are so light that they float easily on water. Every day their parents lead them to safe places to feed. Swans can be very fierce when they are guarding their young. They will attack any animal that comes too close, even humans— so be careful if you see them.

Baby swans are called cygnets. These cygnets are enjoying a ride on their father's back, safe and warm among his feathers.

Reaching for a fish

A pelican chick reaches far inside its parent's beak in search of food. The parent pelican flies along the coast or over lakes and catches lots of fish. It swallows them all and flies home. Then it brings the fish back up for the chick to eat.

Parent peckers

A hungry herring gull chick pecks at the bright red spot at the tip of its parent's beak. This persuades its parent to bring up food for the chick to eat.

Herring gull chicks are not as brightly colored as their parents. This helps them hide from foxes, bigger gulls, and other enemies.

Cup-shaped nests

A bird's nest is where it lays its eggs and raises its young. The nest helps to keep the eggs and baby birds sheltered and warm. Many birds build cup-shaped nests high above the ground in trees.

Chaffinch nest

The chaffinch builds its nest in a small fork in a bush or tree. It is made of grass, moss, and roots, and lined with feathers and hair to keep the eggs warm.

Hard work

The female chaffinch has to make several hundred trips to collect all the right material in order to build a nest. She decorates the outside with lichen, which makes the nest hard to find.

By turning around slowly in the nest, and using its breast to push, the chaffinch makes the cup shape.

A hard bed

Instead of a downy bed, baby song thrushes have to sleep on a hard bed of mud. The song thrush makes a cup-shaped nest of roots, hairs, and grass, then finally adds a thin lining of wet mud.

When the mud dries, it becomes hard and strong.

Mud collector

The female song thrush collects grass, roots, dead leaves, twigs, and also wet mud from puddles.

Nest ingredients

Pieces of sheep's wool, spiders' webs, and even human hair and ribbons have all been found woven into birds' nests.

Pieces of tree bark give a nest strength.

Sheep's wool caught on barbed wire fences makes a warm nest lining.

Mud is picked up from puddles and stream banks.

Twigs and leaves

Strange nests

Not all nests are cup-shaped. Some birds just scrape hollows in the ground. Others use strange materials: tiny cave swiftlets make little cup-shaped nests of their own spit, which hardens as it dries on the cave wall. The mallee fowl builds a huge mound of sand and buries its eggs in the middle.

The chicks live in the round part of the nest.

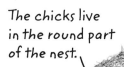

Weaving a home
The male weaver bird starts with a knotted ring hanging from a tree. Then it weaves fresh grass in and out until the nest is completed.

Weaver bird nest
Weavers are birds that make their nests by weaving lots of pieces of grass together. Their nests are light and airy, but also strong and showerproof. The long "tunnel" leading to the nest stops snakes and other predators getting inside to eat the eggs and the young.

Entrance to nest

Dirty work
Cliff swallows make
their nests out of mud pellets.
Collecting the mud can be dirty
work, so they hold their wings and
tails out of the way.

Reedy nest
The reed warbler makes a nest
of fresh grasses, reed flowers,
and feathers in a reed bed.
The Sun dries out both the
nest and the surrounding
reeds, turning them
brown. This makes the
nest harder to see.

Penduline tit nests are so soft
and tightly woven that
children in Eastern Europe
used to wear them as slippers.

Penduline tit nest
The Eurasian penduline tit builds its nest in
birch or willow trees. First, the male makes a
hoop of grass hanging from the tip of a branch.
Then the female helps him build the rest of the
nest, using spiders' webs and moss.

33

Cleaning and preening

Birds must keep their feathers in perfect condition. If they are dirty or ruffled, it is difficult to fly and keep warm, so they need constant care. A good place to watch birds clean their feathers is by a birdbath or a puddle in the park. Afterward, they comb the feathers with their beaks. This is called preening.

The starling uses its beak to zip up the branches, or barbs, of its feathers.

Preening time
The starling runs each ruffled feather through its beak to make them smooth. Then it uses its beak to collect oil from a preen gland at the base of its tail. It wipes the oil over its feathers to condition or waterproof them.

Unzipped, ruffled feather

Zipped up feather

Zipped up
The little branches of each feather have tiny hooks that can be zipped up to make a smooth strong surface for flying.

Splish splash

A good splash in the water is the first step in a bird's cleaning routine. Bathing birds fluff up their feathers, then duck down and use their wings to splash water over their bodies.

A corn bunting keeps an eye out for danger while it washes its feathers.

MAKE A BIRDBATH

You can make a birdbath from a trash-can lid, or plant-pot saucer, and some bricks. Birds need a gentle slope so they can paddle in and out, and a rough surface so they don't slip.

1. Set three bricks in a triangle on flat ground in the open. Put the lid upside down on the bricks. Add a layer of clean small stones and a few larger pebbles. Fill with water.

2. Keep the bath full and make sure the water does not freeze in winter. Rinse it out every so often to keep the water clean.

3. It's important that you place the birdbath away from trees, bushes, or other places where a cat could hide, so it cannot pounce on birds while they are drinking or bathing.

Feeding habits

Birds have many different ways of feeding. Swifts catch insects on the wing. Starlings push their beaks into the soil to seize grubs. Herons use their bills for spearing fish, while finches use their beaks for cracking seeds.

Snail smasher

If you find broken snail shells in your yard, you may have discovered a song thrush's anvil. The thrush smashes open shells on a favorite stone to get the snail inside.

Floating umbrella

When the black heron hunts fish, it lowers its head and neck and spreads its wings around until they meet in front. This shades the water from the sun, making it easier to spot fish.

Acrobatic birds

Tits are the acrobats of the bird world. They are often seen hanging upside down from bird feeders, or from twigs as they search for insects.

FEED THE BIRDS

A feeding bell on a rope attracts chickadees and other tits, and provides a safe feeding place out of reach of cats. To make a feeding bell, you'll need a yogurt cup, a piece of strong string, bird food (seeds, nuts, raisins, crumbs), melted fat (lard, suet, or drippings) and a mixing bowl.

1. Ask an adult to help you make a small hole in the bottom of the cup. Thread the string through and secure it with a large knot or tie a small twig on the end.

2. ASK AN ADULT to warm the fat until it melts. Then mix in the bird food in a bowl.

3. Spoon the mixture into the cup and leave it in a cool place until it hardens.

4. Hang the bell on a tree in the yard or on the side of a bird table. Watch for tits performing as they feed.

Meal in a nutshell

The nuthatch wedges an acorn or hazelnut into a crack in tree bark, then hammers it open to reach the seed inside. If you find a nut shell with a jagged hole or split in two, it will have been eaten by a bird.

Crossed bill

Crossbills have a unique bill that crosses over at the tips. It is designed to prize seeds out of spruce or pinecones, but it can also pick bark off tree trunks to reach insects.

37

Meat-eating birds

There are many meat-eaters in the bird world. The ones that hunt by swooping and attacking with their claws are called birds of prey. Most birds of prey watch out for food from high in the air, so this is the best place to look for them.

Fishing from the air

The majestic bald eagle fishes from the air. It flaps over the water, snatches up a fish in its claws, then flies away with it to a perch. Bald eagles are usually seen near lakes, rivers, and coasts.

The bald eagle uses its huge, hooked beak to pull apart fish and other animals that it catches.

Feathered hunters

Many other birds, such as shrikes, use their beaks rather than their claws to catch small animals and insects. Shrikes store their food by spearing it on long thorns.

Eyes in the sky

Vultures soar high in the sky in search of food. They also keep close watch on each other. When one bird spots a meal, others quickly follow it.

Most vultures have no feathers on their heads, since blood would make their feathers dirty when they feed. The king vulture is unusual because its head is brightly colored.

Pinpointing prey

The kestrel is one of the few birds of prey that can hover. It hangs in the air as it pinpoints its prey, then drops down to catch it in its claws.

Cleaning up

Vultures may not be very popular birds, but they do a very useful job by eating up the remains of dead animals. They peck holes in the carcasses, and stretch out their long necks to feed inside.

Night hunters

When the Sun sets, most birds settle down for the night. Owls are different. Most of them spend the day asleep, and wake up when it gets dark. Owls hunt small animals at night, using their sensitive eyes and ears.

These feathery tufts look like ears, but the real ears are lower down, hidden at the sides of the owl's face.

Owls have "binocular" vision. This means that both their eyes point in the same direction, just like ours. This way of seeing lets an owl know exactly how far away its prey is.

Still life

The long-eared owl spends the day perched motionless on a branch. It is very difficult to see, because its feathers make it look just like a piece of wood. This owl has long "ear" tufts that it can raise or lower. These help it to recognize other owls of the same type, or species.

The barn owl

The barn owl lives all over the world, from America to Australia. Like other owls, it has a bowl-shaped face. This guides sounds into its ears, which are hidden under its feathers.

The barn owl catches small animals with its claws, then carries them off in its beak. It swallows them whole.

Owls can see their prey by moonlight, or even by starlight.

WHAT'S ON THE MENU?

After an owl has eaten, it coughs up a pellet. This contains the bones and fur of its prey. Old pellets are quite safe to handle, and you can gently pull them apart with tweezers to see what an owl has been eating. The best place to look for pellets is in old barns, or around tree trunks.

Hipbone

Jawbones

Skull

Vole leg bones

Owl pellet

Bird territories

The world of birds is full of private property—pieces of land called territories. They are an important part of the way many birds live. By claiming a territory, a bird can make sure that it has somewhere to attract a mate, a place to nest, and enough space for a growing family.

Bird song
To us, bird song is just a pretty sound. To birds, however, it is a way of sending messages about their territories.

Eastern bluebirds sing from high perches so that they can be heard a long way off.

It's my yard!
Male European robins often set up territories in gyards. The owner sings loudly to tell other robins where his territory is. If another male robin flies into the territory, a battle quickly follows.

LISTEN AND LEARN
Most types of bird have a distinctive song or call. You will often hear a bird before you see it. Try recording birds singing on a smartphone or tablet. In some countries, you can download an app that will help you identify a bird from its song.

The female will mate with the male who puts on the best performance.

Each male sits on a different branch, which is his territory. The displaying male bows and flaps its wings.

Forest showground

Male Andean cock-of-the-rocks gather in an arena of trees to display for watching females. They show off their feathers and squawk loudly.

Keep your distance

Gannets are large seabirds that nest together on rocky cliffs and islands. Around each nest is a small territory, reaching just as far as the bird on the nest can stretch.

Pairs of nesting gannets have to stay beyond the "pecking distance" of their neighbors.

Flying away

Have you noticed how some birds disappear in winter? Have you ever wondered where they go? Many spend their lives in two different places. They spend winter where it is warmer. Then in spring, they fly away to raise their families where there is plenty of food. These journeys are migrations.

Flight of the snow goose
The snow goose breeds in the Arctic tundra, and migrates south to the Gulf of Mexico. Its journey is about 2,000 miles (3,200 km) long. The world's greatest bird traveler, the Arctic tern, on average makes a two-way trip of 43,500 miles (70,000 km) between the Arctic and Antarctic every year.

Wild geese migrate in V-shaped flocks. Flying in this formation uses less energy. Each bird gets a lift from the force of the bird in front.

COUNTING THE BIRDS

Here is a quick way to count the birds in a migrating flock. Make a circle with your thumb and index finger. Hold your arm out, and count the birds in the circle. Then see roughly how many circles it takes to cover the whole flock. Multiply the first number by the second to get the answer.

Herald of summer

According to an old English saying, "one swallow doesn't make a summer." But when barn swallows arrive, you can be sure that summer is not far behind. In fall, young swallows migrate with their parents. The following spring, many find their way from southern Africa back to Europe by instinct.

Traveling geese

Barnacle geese travel in flocks that can contain thousands of birds. They pause on their long journey to rest and feed at their favorite lakes. At night, you can hear the geese calling as they fly overhead. They use the Sun and stars as a compass to help them find their way.

45

Birds of the sea

Many seabirds make their homes on rocky cliffs, where they are safer from their enemies. Each bird has its favorite nesting place. The puffin likes grassy slopes at the top of cliffs, while gannets are quite happy on bare rock. Seabirds often spend the winter months far out at sea and come ashore to breed.

Diving gannets

Gannets feed on fish such as mackerel and herring. A gannet has a special shock-absorbing layer under its skin. This protects it when it dives into the water.

Gannets always breed together, in groups of up to 50,000 nests.

Gannets dive headfirst into the sea to catch fish. They fold their wings back before they hit the water.

Clifftop clowns

With their large, striped beaks and bright orange feet, puffins are hard to miss. They tunnel in soft ground on grassy slopes and islands, and catch fish out at sea.

Short wings

Puffins can hold lots of fish at once in their beaks.

Webbed feet spread out for landing

Puffins use old rabbit burrows as nests or dig burrows for themselves using their beaks.

Perched on the edge

The guillemot (gill-i-mot) makes no nest at all, but lays its single egg on a cliff ledge. The parent bird holds the egg in its feet. Guillemots nest in big, noisy colonies.

The guillemot's egg is pear-shaped, so that it rolls around in a circle instead of falling off the cliff.

Birds of the shore

Sandy beaches are fine for swimming and sunbathing, but if you want to watch shore birds, the thing to look for is lots of sticky mud. Muddy shores contain a hidden world of small animals, from worms to tiny snails, and many different kinds of birds feed on them. Most of these birds are waders, which means they have long legs and probing beaks.

Beak with a bend

You don't have to be the world's smartest birdwatcher to recognize an avocet, because it is one of the few birds with a beak that curves upward.

The Eurasian avocet moves its beak from side to side in the water, snapping it shut when it feels food.

Although it can swim, the avocet usually strides through the water on its long legs. Its legs are so long that they trail behind the avocet when it flies.

A feast in the mud

The bar-tailed godwit reaches deep into the mud with its long beak, which snaps open and shut just like a pair of tweezers.

The stone turner

Flocks of turnstones can be seen walking along the shore in search of food. These small birds turn over stones with their probing beaks, hoping to find crabs and other small animals.

Strong, orange beak

Shell-smasher

If you have ever collected seashells, you will know how tough they are. However, small shells are no match for the oystercatcher. With sharp blows of its strong, rodlike beak, it smashes them open and eats the soft animal inside.

Anything goes

Some birds are very choosy about what they eat, but the herring gull will feed on almost anything. Dead fish, baby birds, earthworms, and rotting trash are all on the menu when it looks for food.

The herring gull uses its powerful beak to pull apart its food, and also to peck its way to the front in the scramble to eat.

Freshwater birds

Ponds, streams, rivers, and lakes are often teeming with small animals and plants. Tiny fish, young insects, shrimp, and waterweed are all food for freshwater birds. Most of these birds feed by swimming on the surface or diving, while others wade through the shallows. However, kingfishers catch small fish by diving at them from a perch.

Ducks and drakes
Mallards live on ponds, lakes, and streams. The male is called the "drake" and has a shiny green head. The female is called the "duck" and is drab and brown.

Drake

Duck

Tail in the air
Mallards feed in two ways. They either "up end" to reach food just below the surface, or they scoop small animals and plants off the surface.

Attack from the air

A good place to see a kingfisher is from a bridge. Here you can watch it darting up and down a stream or a river. A kingfisher spells danger to small fish. Once it catches a fish, it bashes its prey against a perch to stun it, then swallows the whole fish headfirst.

You can recognize a Eurasian kingfisher by its bright turquoise feathers.

Kingfishers make nests in riverbank burrows. They peck away at the soil, then kick out the pieces.

The kingfisher plunges in headfirst to catch a fish in its beak.

The roseate spoonbill's special diet makes its feathers pink.

A beak with two spoons

It is easy to see how spoonbills got their name. The ends of their beaks are broad and round, just like a pair of spoons. A spoonbill wades slowly through the water with its beak half-open and waves it from side-to-side. When it feels food, its two "spoons" close around it.

Woodland birds

Hundreds of different birds live in woods, and trees make safe homes for them. They build their nests high up among the leaves, or hidden inside hollow trunks. A good place to wait for birds is near a clearing, where you can spot them feeding on insects and seeds.

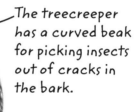

The treecreeper has a curved beak for picking insects out of cracks in the bark.

Tree climber

The treecreeper travels up and around tree trunks looking for food. It usually only climbs upward. When it reaches the top, it flies to the bottom of the next tree and starts all over again.

The treecreeper uses its stiff tail as a prop for hopping up tree trunks.

Acorns away

The acorn woodpecker wedges acorns firmly into the bark of a favorite tree to make a winter food-store.

Woodpecker warning

You might hear this woodpecker before you see it! With its powerful beak, it drums loudly on dead wood to proclaim its territory. Woodpeckers also use their beaks to make nest holes in trees, and to drill into rotten tree trunks in search of grubs to eat.

The hairy woodpecker sits on its tail when it feeds its young.

Hidden in the leaves

The nightjar comes out at night to feed on moths. By day, it sits perfectly still on the rough ground. Its feathers match the dead leaves so well that it is almost impossible to spot the bird.

Forgotten trees

In fall, look for jays collecting acorns. They bury them in the ground to eat later. However, the birds forget many of the hiding places, and in spring the acorns sprout into little oak trees.

Desert and grassland birds

Many hot desert and grassland birds seek shelter from the Sun's heat during the hottest part of the day, and a few only appear at night. However, in the daytime, watch for large birds high in the sky, and for flocks of small birds flitting around in search of seeds and insects. At sunrise and sunset, look out for desert birds at water holes.

Full speed ahead

America's roadrunner literally runs across the desert chasing lizards and snakes. It can reach speeds of 12 mph (20 kph). When in danger, it prefers to run rather than fly.

Thirsty chicks

Sandgrouse often fly as far as 19 miles (30 km) across the desert to find water. They have special breast feathers that soak up large amounts of water. The male sandgrouse soaks his feathers in a pool or water hole, then flies home. The thirsty chicks suck the water from his feathers.

The ostrich is the world's fastest two-legged runner. It can run at speeds of up to 45 mph (70 kph).

Female ostriches are brown.

Snake stalker

The secretary bird builds a nest of twigs and dead branches on the top of a thorn tree. This long-legged bird of prey stalks the grassland in search of snakes to eat, then bites off their heads before taking them home to feed to its chicks.

Big bird

Ostriches wander across dry African grasslands in search of food and water. They are the largest birds in the world. Some stand over 8 ft (2.5m) tall.

Ostriches are too big to fly, but their long legs carry them away from danger.

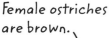

Tropical birds

You will see some of the most colorful birds in the world's tropical forests. Parrots and toucans live in the treetops, and male birds-of-paradise display their beautiful feathers to attract mates. Jungle fowl and pheasants roam the forest floor and hummingbirds hover at flowers, while eagles soar high overhead.

On the lookout

This sulfur-crested cockatoo is on guard duty. "Guards" stay up in the trees while the rest of the flock eats seeds on the ground. If there is any sign of danger, they will shriek a loud warning.

What toucans do

Toucans fly around the more open areas of tropical forests, calling out to each other with loud froglike croaks. They nest in small tree holes and may use the same site the following year.

The toucan uses its huge beak to reach fruit hanging from branches.

Brilliant colors

There are lots of parrots in tropical forests. They use their strong hooked beaks to crack open nuts. Their beaks can also be useful when climbing around in trees. Parrots usually fly around in small groups. Listen for their harsh cries, and look for their brilliant colors as they fly overhead.

A long tail helps this crimson rosella from Australia to balance as it twists and turns between the trees.

You can recognize the male jungle fowl by the large red "comb" on his head.

Tropical chickens

Asia's red jungle fowl is the domestic chicken's wild ancestor. Like chickens, jungle fowl live on the ground, where they scrape around for seeds.

The female jungle fowl has dull colors to hide her while she sits on her eggs on the forest floor.

City birds

Many birds—starlings, sparrows, pigeons, and even gulls—have learned to live with people. Small birds such as robins, tits, finches, and thrushes nest in hidden corners of city gardens, and peregrine falcons raise their young on tall buildings. In winter, watch for unusual visitors moving in from the country to feed on berries, rotting apples, and bird-table food.

Messy birds

City pigeons roost and nest on the ledges of buildings. Their droppings mess up city streets and statues, and are expensive to clean up.

Summer visitors

House martins build their mud nests under the eaves of city roofs. You can often spot their little white faces peering out. House martins are summer visitors to Europe, arriving in late April. After they have reared their young, they return to Africa in late September.

The house martin makes its nest out of mud. Sticky wet mud helps to glue the nest into position.

NEST BOXES

Many birds that nest in holes in trees in the wild will happily use wooden nest boxes in city gardens instead. You can help garden birds by putting up your own nest boxes on suitable trees or posts. They need to have a small opening just large enough for the birds to squeeze inside.

City scavengers

Magpies feed on almost anything, including scraps of food dropped on the street, and the eggs and young of smaller birds. Pigeons and thrushes often attack magpies to keep them away from their nests.

Look for the white crescent on a magpie's back as it flies.

Index

Acknowledgments

**Dorling Kindersley
would like to thank:**

Simon Battensby for
photography on pages
10 and 12.
Sharon Grant and Faith
Nelson for design assistance.
Gin von Noorden and Kate
Rasworth for editorial
assistance and research.
Hilary Bird for the index.
Kim Taylor for special
photography on pages
14–15, 23, 24–25, 26–27, 52.

31901060309848